MOUNTAIN
Style

MOUNTAIN
Style

Mary Whitesides

Photographs by Matthew Reier

Salt Lake City

First Edition

05 04 03 02 01   5 4 3 2 1

Published by
Gibbs Smith, Publisher
P.O. Box 667
Layton, UT 84041

Orders: (1-800) 748-5439
www.gibbs-smith.com

Designed by Cherie Hanson
Edited by Gail Yngve

Printed and bound in Hong Kong

Library of Congress Cataloging-in-Publication Data

Whitesides, Mary.
Mountain style / Mary Whitesides.— 1st ed.
p. cm.
ISBN 1-58685-040-7
1. Interior decoration—Rocky Mountains Region. 2. Decoration and
ornament, Rustic—Rocky Mountains Region. 3. Interior decoration
accessories—Rocky Mountains Region. I. Title.
NK2004 .W49 2001
747.218—dc21
2001001923

CONTENTS

INTRODUCTION
For Purple Mountain Majesties~   10

THE ROCKY MOUNTAINS~
Past & Present   14

MOUNTAIN
Architecture & Decor   24

THE NEW MOUNTAIN
Style   30

CONTEMPORARY
Rustic   36

JACKSON HOLE
Elegance   44

THE HEALING POWERS
of the Mountain   56

A "TREE"
House   66

VICTORIAN
Charm   76

AN ATYPICAL
Lodge   84

A *LITTLE* LOG CABIN
in the Woods   94

HIGH-ELEVATION
Southwestern Style   104

NATURE'S
Garden   112

Acknowledgments

It is clear that a book like this is not a solo project nor could one single person execute it. I would like to thank the many people, businesses, and institutions that have made *Mountain Style* a reality.

I wish to thank the photographers for taking a leap of faith with me and believing in the book. Without Matthew Reier, photographer, and his assistant, Paul Winder, these beautiful photographs would not exist. The project was ambitious and we couldn't cover it all, so thanks also go to Gregg Bauman, Ralph J. Ribicic, Judi Boisson, Doug Williams, Dave LaMure, Bob Hills, Steve Young, Darcy Foreman, and Sundance Catalog Company for their contributions. And finally, thank you to Debra Macfarlane for the author photograph.

Special thanks to all architects, interior designers, friends, and homeowners who helped me locate the beautiful homes featured in the book, especially architects Nancy Carney of Carney Architects; Von B. White; John C. Shirley and Associates; and Gary Francis; and interior designers Jo Ann Mullen, Eva Klein, Brian Goff, Pat Harker, Alice Soohoo, and Tom Jones.

My gratitude goes to Lyndsay Rowan and Cecilia Heffernan for their cooperation. Special thanks to Ruth and John Sundberg and Kathy Wilson for help in finding special mountain homes. The homeowners were so open and gracious, allowing us to invade their homes and lives for photographs. I thank them.

For research materials, I am grateful to Sun Valley Chamber of Commerce, Sun Valley, Idaho; Aspen Historical Society, Aspen, Colorado; Jackson Hole Historical Society, Jackson Hole, Wyoming; and the Historical Society in Red Lodge, Montana; and my mother, Leah Chappell, for the article from the Daughters of the Utah Pioneers on Park City, Utah.

Park City Writers Group gave me great suggestions and encouragement, especially C. J. Johnson and Corinne Humphreys. And, as always, thanks to my family for their interest and support.

The informal eclectic style of this vestibule off a master bedroom invites one to write in a journal or become engrossed in a mystery novel. Covered in antique velvet brocade, the chair from the Flying Trunk is complemented by a traditional tray table from India.

For Purple Mountain Majesties

—Katharine Lee Bates

I grew up at the foot of the Rocky Mountains. They were rugged, secure and always there. The peaks spoke to me in more ways than one. I could contemplate for hours a roiling storm gathering over God's own temples. He and Zeus must have had some fine arguments. When the jagged swords had all been flung and the roaring voices finished clashing, those mountains, drenched with rain or snow, were either blessed with wildflowers or left pristine as a wedding dress. And always, they invited my soul. Whether it was for a time of quiet contemplation or a playful melding of nature and fun, I came away relaxed and renewed.

In those days, mountain-shaped A-frame houses mimicked European retreats. The high-pitched roofs and glass walls allowed nature to pour through the dwelling. On many hikes, I threaded through those mini mountain structures neighboring on antique miners' cabins to reach the trails.

These whimsical glass flower candlesticks come from a long tradition of glass-bead making in Ghana, West Africa—an Aid to Artisans project.

The glacial lakes were fine for a five-minute skinny-dip, the mountain trails a safari through bear country, and the snowy slopes a glide of freedom the spirit shared with the body. Quiet time on a boulder provided answers to life's little curves.

Like many curious and adventurous people, I moved away to experience new horizons. I spent a decade and a half in the man-made mountains of New York City. The urban sophistication of man's achievements filled my thirst for culture, and the lack of nature encouraged me to explore the nuances of my fellowman. I absorbed and drank in all that I could. After a while, like a glass nearly full but missing a certain well-known flavor, I sought the rolling hills of New England to find that elusive element. I found so much charm, so much history, but not the peaks that left an engraved imprint on my heart. With a great love for two different ways of life, I set out to combine both the refined East and the rugged West.

Cotton canvas is hand screened with an antique photograph, and then appliqued on a chenille pillow, becoming art to look at and lean on.

I am fully aware that this is not a new idea. Over the past century many sophisticated, moneyed, and/or adventurous Americans have done just that. The famous "Go West, young man" was a testimonial. If it weren't for many easterners, such as Rockefeller and Roosevelt, who heeded the call, much of the West would not have been preserved for our pleasure.

Today, people from all over the U.S. migrate to the mountains. Because of urban sprawl, we rarely experience the sensation of our feet upon the bare earth any more. Skyscrapers have blocked our eyes from nature, and noise has deadened the music of the birds. People who have never before lived near nature's cathedrals are finding what I found in my youth—that they harbor hidden treasures: pure water, clean air, and wildlife. Many people still have a romantic notion of going where nobody else has gone. It's the gallantry of the explorer spirit and the tribulations of the tenderfoot. In the mountains, we feel hardy, healthy, and invigorated with a newfound connection to nature. The scenery is a painting for our eyes, the air a lung elixir. Standing closer to heaven, we are encompassed by an earthly playground.

With unprecedented connection to each other through the media, people of this century are exposed to outdoor adventure rarely experienced firsthand. We question the practicality of a 4 x 4 SUV four-wheelin' on the streets of Manhattan. Western decor in a city apartment can be an instant reprieve from city life, but more often we are melding sophisticated and rustic styles as city dwellers embrace wildflowers and pine trees on western slopes. Moving west in record numbers, they bring with them their sleek high-rise furnishings. This is not unlike ancestors in the 1800s bringing precious family heirlooms in covered wagons. Today, that blend of the refined and the raw has created a new look I call *Mountain Style*. I invite you to explore this new style from your armchair. Perhaps the mountains will inspire you somehow as they have writers, poets, artists, architects, designers, naturalists, and all manner of people who have stood before them and found humility. ▼

CHAPTER ONE

THE ROCKY MOUNTAINS—Past & Present

THE ROCKY MOUNTAINS–
Past & Present

Evidence has shown that people lived 10,000 years ago in the Rocky Mountains during the Ice Age. It was the land that sustained them, and thousands of years later the Indians followed plant cycles and game migrations to survive there as well. Mountain men such as Jim Bridger invaded the same territory to establish the fur trade. A series of rendezvous under open log structures served as central places to bring pelts for trade. The mountains became a means for commerce.

By 1850, hundreds of people came to the mountains to uncover hidden treasures. "Thar's gold in them thar hills" set off a frenzy of overnight boomtowns in the western Rockies. Many people prospered and built homes and cities. From small shacks to opera houses, these cities evolved from shantytowns to cultural centers. But people's luck ran out when silver prices fell and most of the communities became ghost towns. After lying dormant like a tulip bulb in a closet for a number of years, the European idea of mountain and nature as playground was the impetus for those towns slowly to bloom again. Early miners fought the elements to survive; contemporary residents have sought those same elements for pleasure. Frontiersmen who found a fortune in the mountains

removed it and left, finding the life too simple. Modern-day settlers have invested their wealth paying a premium for that simple life.

Life could not have been simpler in the early 1800s than in the tent cities pitched by explorers and prospectors with big dreams. Canvas communities, full of transient fortune seekers, disappointed some but rewarded many. Those who uncovered evidence of silver or gold soon replaced their flimsy cloth cocoons with more permanent structures. The miners, most of them bachelors, built cabins randomly on the mountains with found materials such as logs, stone, mud, straw, and metal. Homeowners were considered well-off if they had a shingled roof and paid $200 for such a house. Most of the shacks had roofs made of straw and mud. Some occupants had an open umbrella inside to keep dry. Clothes were hidden in covered rain barrels used for closets. Snowfall could be so heavy that entire settlements were lost regularly to snow-storms and avalanches.

The young and adventurous filled these boom-towns. Their energy established a lifestyle full of saloons and all-night parties. The partygoers' children were bedded down on log benches. In

ABOVE: In the hands of a fine artist, antlers have been transformed into sculpture. Harker Designs has secured a variety of shapes from this artist.

LEFT: Steve Young of Hammerton honors the texture of branches forever preserved on this metal fire screen.

The elegance of antiquity is reproduced on this sofa with modern comfort and style in mind. The leather bench is used as a coffee table or doubles for extra seating.

addition, all the classic images of the Wild West were lived and played out in these settlements. Saloon shootouts, bank robberies, lynchings, and mine explosions—all fodder for legend—were romanticized in the movies. Posse hunts were the precursors of the classic car chase.

An entourage of multinational citizens added to the social structure. The Cornish and Scots were miners; the English, businessmen; the Chinese, cooks, launderers, farmers, and builders; and the Scandinavians, lumberjacks and skiers. All of them left a cultural mark.

Artist John Gallis, whose work is shown at the Martin-Harris Gallery, crafts free-form walnut timber into a bench and civilizes it with a leather cushion.

As a means of breaking free from the dark dreary mines and the drudgery of mundane occupations, the men concentrated on organized baseball games, horse races, boxing matches, and skiing for recreation. The ladies enjoyed tea, crumpets, and culture, setting up art exhibits, operas, plays, and the first moving-picture theaters. No question they were comfortable letting men wear the pants. Females caught on the streets in such garb would have been arrested anyway. But the sexes met on common ground at the ice-skating rink, bringing together sports and socials.

Out of necessity, people got around on snowshoes, or Norwegian skis about nine feet long. The U.S. Postal Service used these skis to deliver the mail. Skiing became sport for the adventurous. Hiking treacherous terrain to reach the desired height took all day for one run down the mountain, picnic lunch included.

The Victorian era brought grace to the Rockies. With that polish came fine buildings of hand-split stone and brick stabilized by hand-hewn beams. As refined as the towns became, the very wealthy invested their money elsewhere. Real-estate prices were not the issue in 1893, as land sold at one penny an acre. The harsh living conditions did not interest folks back then.

People like George Hearst (William Randolph's father) made a fortune in silver mining. That money built the famous San Simeon Castle and funded the Hearst newspaper empire. By the early 1900s, however, luck was running out and many upstart communities became near ghost towns. The federal government devalued the price of silver, and the bottom fell out of the market. Citizens jumped ship in this sinking economy, leaving houses and buildings boarded up. But the seeds for recreational commerce had already been planted, eventually defining a new economic base.

The first developers were private families, building makeshift log cabins to rent to seasonal workers. Like many grassroots movements, the concept of retreat in these cabins caught the eye of the adventurous. Charles Lindbergh practiced flying and tested mountain air patterns. Calamity Jane, the Sundance Kid, and Buffalo Bill all came to the Rockies and used the same cabins for recreation and renewal.

Struggling ranchers saw the economic potential and came up with the concept of "dude ranch." The summer months attracted would-be cowboys enjoying a respite from city traffic and noise. By 1920, fine hunting lodges were built and visited by the rich and famous seeking the excitement of tracking game. In the fall months, men of wealth came to hunt much the same way they went on safari in Africa. (Hemingway based the coroner in *For Whom the Bell Tolls* on his western hunting guide.) Others enjoyed fishing and pack trips. Selfish about their discovery, no one wanted roads marked or paved, preferring the isolation.

The winter months held a different kind of potential recreation. The famous Tenth Mountain Division used the mountains for a snowy training ground during World War II, and many soldiers vowed to come back after the war was over. And—they did—developing ski lifts, ski runs, shops, and restaurants.

Europeans influenced Averell Harriman, chairman of the Union Pacific board of directors in the 1930s, to establish America's first destination ski resort. He wanted lavish accommodations and hired the finest architects to ensure the same splendor as the landscape. With excellent cuisine and contemporary entertainment in place, he had his railroad engineers design the first chair lift, based on a hoist used to haul bananas from ships' holds. During the next forty years, many developments followed.

The first lodge had bunks where skiers brought their own sleeping bags. Victorian hotel rooms rented for $1.50 per night and, by 1930, $3.00 per night. Today, lodge rates start at more than $100 a night, and the ski industry has become a recreational spiderweb, binding prosperity and pleasure. Now the world romps together in the mountains, sharing the best of all scenarios whether it's winter or summer.

From prehistoric men to tent cities and miners' log cabins to Swiss chalets—contemporary architecture and interior design have evolved in the Rocky Mountains by incorporating the nostalgia of the past, the technology of the present, and the imagination of the future. ▼

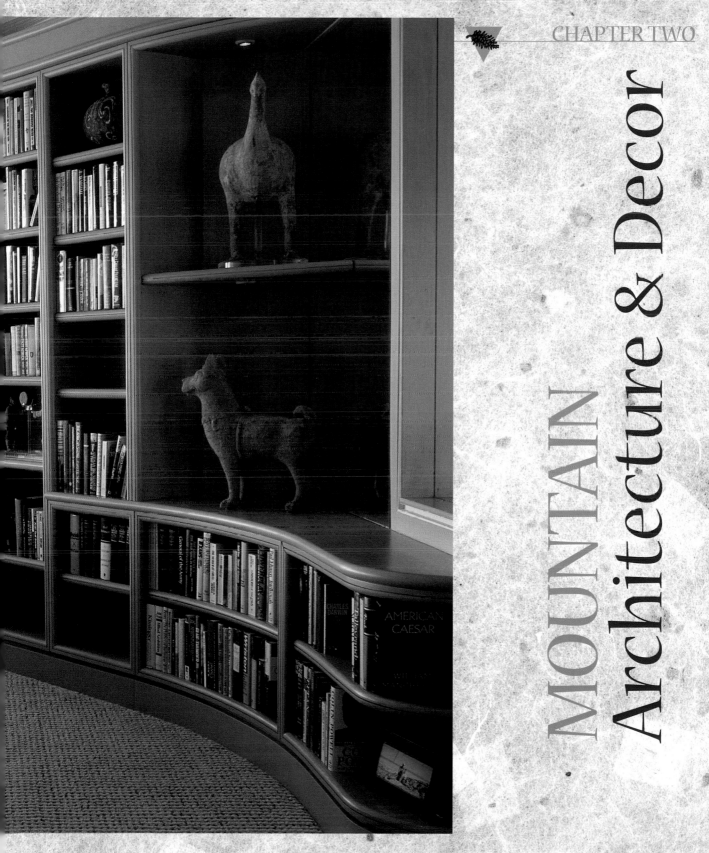

CHAPTER TWO

MOUNTAIN
Architecture & Decor

MOUNTAIN
Architecture & Decor

The idea of "home" now brings with it traditional as well as futuristic criteria for nesting. Technical servicing and multiple opportunities in prosperous times have changed our lives. We can choose where we want to live, and many people have the option of a second home.

Most fine craftsmen, architects, and designers have learned from the past. One of the best qualities can be the patina that comes with age, giving depth and charm to a structure. True creativity is achieved through the marriage of past, present, and future. In the mountains, weathered materials, aged over time or by a man-made process, are blended with technically precise components to produce exciting new architectural and design elements. Materials such as weathered beams, hand-chiseled stone, river rock, antique metals, and hand-hewn log columns are reminiscent of the past. Today's honed granite, stained concrete, refined mahogany, stainless steel, and copper blended with items recycled from the past homogenize beautifully into a rustic-modern look.

New construction methods are as different from the old as a wagon is from a rocket. Back in the 1800s, an avalanche easily took out miners' shacks, sliding them down the hill or crushing them with heavy snow. Log cabins were a sturdy alternative but had leaking roofs. Old stone structures could have benefited from radiant heat to prevent the saying "stone cold." And clapboard Victorian homes had crooked floors from wood checking and shifting that caused cold drafts if not corrected by the newspaper stuck in cracks.

The clean simple lines on this arched headboard could be used in a contemporary home, but upholstered in leather it suits a mountain home quite well. The bench, conveniently located for shoe tying, doubles as the footboard.

Building innovations have eliminated the discomfort and unpredictability of weather in mountain living. Today's houses are built with kiln-dried wood and installed with precision tools. Log homes have steep-pitched roofs, double layered to create dead air space and prevent heat loss. Steel framing conforms to weight-bearing codes that carry heavy snow loads. Large Styrofoam blocks filled with concrete are called "leave-in-place" concrete forms and take care of structure and insulation in one step. In addition, new finishes, materials, and furniture embellish the interiors of mountain homes and blend the past with the present, a milestone in the evolution of the domestic circle.

Vaulted barn-like ceilings with hefty old beams, reclaimed plank flooring, and combinations of marble counters, pine cabinets, and stone accents all represent natural mountain opulence. The elegance of glass and steel may be softened with sandblasted wood siding pickled by vinegar and lime. Concrete floors are warmed by radiant heat and stained in rustic colors.

Leather furniture is a common denominator in mountain décor, ranging from fine calfskin to sanded, stained, embossed, or cracked cowhide. Usually, at least one piece of leather furniture will be found somewhere in the house. Barn-wood tables inlaid with rusted-tin ceiling tiles may sit on a refined collector's carpet.

Animal themes often crop up on candlesticks, stair railings, and barstools. Woven twigs may have been borrowed from Adirondack style, but the western woven-twig look is a far cry from the eastern mountain-camp look. Moose, deer, and bears—the prominent wildlife—are honored in tasteful iron sculptural candleholders, paper-towel holders, or doorbells. The wonder and glory of it all is how these elements, and more, translate to one's own personal taste and individuality. ▼

CHAPTER THREE

THE NEW MOUNTAIN *Style*

Like the finest leather saddle, this chair will mold its comfort around an invited guest. Traditionally, leather such as this makes a mountain statement like no other. Trimmed in pounded-metal tacks, the chair only improves with age.

THE NEW MOUNTAIN
Style

An unusual amount of vision and craftsmanship has emerged over the past few years in the home-furnishings business. The nesting phenomenon and the second-home market have galvanized an explosion in creativity. The beauty of talent is that it inspires an imaginative network of ideas like the petals of a blossoming rose. That and the desire of the consumer to be surrounded by the unusual make this an exciting time to personalize a home. Materials and elements are being used in new ways.

Designers and homeowners are taking chances that go way beyond the idea of classics in the Mountain West. Our grandmothers would not have found embossed and rusted tin beautiful on the door of an armoire or barn wood appropriate for furniture. Grandfather might have thought weathered leather proper for a saddle but not on his favorite chair. The blacksmith—content to make horseshoes and garden gates—couldn't fathom a beautiful stool adorned with deer, delicate metal leaves twined around a lamp, or steel pinecones on a fire screen.

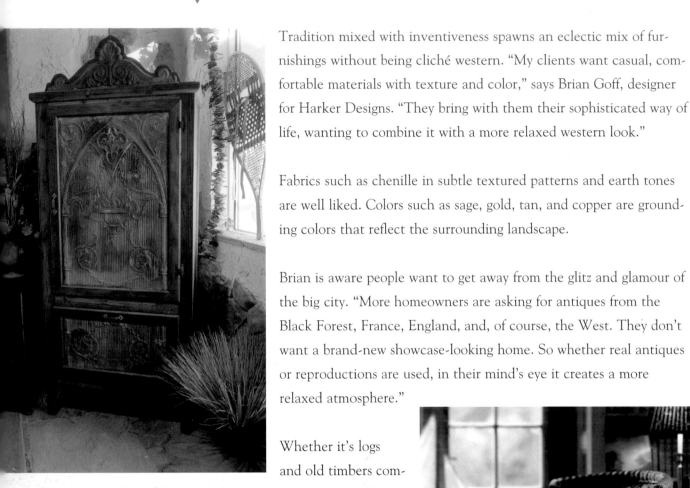

Tradition mixed with inventiveness spawns an eclectic mix of furnishings without being cliché western. "My clients want casual, comfortable materials with texture and color," says Brian Goff, designer for Harker Designs. "They bring with them their sophisticated way of life, wanting to combine it with a more relaxed western look."

Fabrics such as chenille in subtle textured patterns and earth tones are well liked. Colors such as sage, gold, tan, and copper are grounding colors that reflect the surrounding landscape.

Brian is aware people want to get away from the glitz and glamour of the big city. "More homeowners are asking for antiques from the Black Forest, France, England, and, of course, the West. They don't want a brand-new showcase-looking home. So whether real antiques or reproductions are used, in their mind's eye it creates a more relaxed atmosphere."

Embossed metal on the doors of this armoire makes an ordinary piece extraordinary. Exuding character, it's perfect for a mountain home-entertainment center. From Natural Instincts.

Whether it's logs and old timbers combined with marble and limestone, a soft refined chenille sofa next to a worn leather club chair, or an antique armoire housing high-tech equipment, one can get a sense the Old West is still alive and nature still revered. But both are being enjoyed on new terms. ▼

CHAPTER FOUR

CONTEMPORARY Rustic

CONTEMPORARY
Rustic

The unassuming architecture of this capacious house tucked into the aspen trees is full of surprises, with multilevel entrances and hidden skylights. The board and batten exterior will age over time until the wood has the enriched texture of reclaimed timber. Earth-toned dry-stack limestone on the base and fireplace is as elegant as a sculpture. The urbanity of its clean lines suits the ideals of the prosperous tech generation and promises a low-key profile for privacy.

"I have a lot of younger clients from the tech world that want an upbeat kind of rustic," designer Jo Ann Mullen states. "They are looking for something a little more hip." The opportunity to be on the cusp of a contemporary rustic trend opens all kinds of avenues for departure from traditional mountain style. "Very rarely am I working with previously owned furnishings. These people are second and third homeowners looking to start from scratch and move in turnkey."

To accommodate guests, two and three master bedrooms are required, and bigger common areas where children can gather are all based on ski-in, ski-out mentality. Jo Ann studies how the family interacts within the home and bases the seating area in the great room on a relaxing atmosphere in which children and guests can visit without thought of formality. She doesn't use antiques because of her clients' desire for a more contemporary look but incorporates natural elements for tactile accents. "I use rock, wood, and iron with the idea of bringing nature inside. It makes the house user-friendly."

Most of the time people want darker richer woods, such as stained alder and hickory, for more character, combined with stone and slate. In this house, lighter blond woods, slates, and limestone were used to achieve that contemporary look. Textured walls are getting tiresome but are still popular. "I'm having fun experimenting with the new wallpapers," Jo Ann says, "and we are always trying to reinvent faux finishes."

Gathering around the family room fireplace after a hard day of skiing is more than

solace. Gazing into a fire surrounded by magnificent trunks figured by nature is akin to being in an art gallery. A juniper log, gnarled and seasoned, is an illustrious mantelpiece. The use of juniper is newly renowned in mountain décor. Nothing in the room is precious so children can enjoy themselves without reprimands.

The all-wood kitchen is glorified by the use of granite countertops and set off by a ceiling-height shelf. The room is inordinately large to accommodate entertaining of guests. There are two dishwashers and two stoves—one convection and the other gas. The room is open and interactive with the great room.

The alder-wood table has a light stain on it with a slightly distressed surface. The subtly carved detail on the three-inch table edge resembles mountains. Rather than using a traditional turned base or trestle look, Jo Ann wanted to repeat the triangular shape with the legs, and the size can be increased as needed with the insertion of a leaf.

In one of the three master suites is a bed with all the convenience of a hospital stay. But the chipped-paint finish and funky wheels on the rolling tray table takes it far from something that sterile. One never has to leave the bed—it's all set for eating, reading, or working.

ABOVE: Mountains are mimicked here in the wrapped-wire candlesticks from Natural Instincts. The alder table follows the theme with a surprise triangular detail around the edge.

BELOW: The convenience of a tray table on wheels could inspire a dreamer to compose a novel while lingering over breakfast in bed.

Across from the bed, a seating area provides another option for a relaxing afternoon in front of a fireplace. The chipped and carved edge on the limestone mantel creates a controlled natural appearance.

A sizable master bath is light and airy with multiple windows. The issue was privacy and the solution a beautiful etched window. Iron tree branches designed by Jo Ann bring the outdoors inside and function as dresser lights.

The cabinet in this powder room resembles a piece of furniture and is topped with an unlikely counter surface. A large sandstone slab is sealed to prevent stains. The unusual textured walls look like nature's wallpaper. Jo Ann collected these stones on the beach during a vacation, not knowing what she would use them for. She worked right along with the plaster contractor and created the design on-site. ▼

CHAPTER FIVE

JACKSON HOLE Elegance

JACKSON HOLE
Elegance

Adamant about saving as many trees as possible, the architects and owners of this spectacular stone house tucked it neatly in a cottonwood grove and then planted Engelmann spruce to fill in the site. Unlike the western romantic vision often desired by second-home owners, a sense of sophistication and personal lifestyle gave birth to this elegant structure as a permanent residence. Yet it fits comfortably in a western valley setting surrounded by Rocky Mountain peaks. Though it is more common to find combinations of timber and stone in the Mountain West, the option here was for stone.

The exterior stone surfaces create unusual slabs of color and texture interpreted in a refined Craftsman style. Rough-cut stacked limestone forms the base structure. In contrast the upper portion is veneered Colorado sandstone. Sensitive to the solar path, the house is deliberately oriented for southern exposure, ensuring the living areas the warmest option. Windows set north to the mountain peaks provide beauty lovers an unprecedented view. But it is a beauty that can sometimes be harsh during winter months.

Tightly insulated, the walls have an R factor of 38, attributable to the leave-in-place concrete forms. Huge Styrofoam blocks with a void are filled with concrete, forming the structure and creating insulation simultaneously. None of the skeletal engineering is faulty underneath the rainbow of stone and metal cladding.

Architect Nancy Carney says, "I was purely having fun solving the facing for a curved wall. The copper sheet engraved by a local craftsman will weather beautifully over time with nature's brush."

The interior is an uncluttered masterpiece of blended materials and colors. A soft beige limestone tile is not disappointing to the eye in the entrance, and a grand descent down an elegant staircase stirs the imagination, distracted only by the scene out the three-story windows across the living room. To the left, a curious hallway leading to the kitchen becomes a conservatory space that opens into an English garden. On the right, a formal dining room can be contained behind copper-wrapped sliding doors.

ABOVE: The Arts & Crafts entrance here is a rich blend of mahogany, Colorado limestone, and burnished copper.

LEFT: A hallway space becomes a place to pause and contemplate an English garden.

The kitchen gives new meaning to the cliché "dream kitchen." Combined in one open space with an entertainment/seating area, it becomes a natural sanctuary for family and friends. The concrete floors are warmed by a deep rust-red stain that complements the mahogany cabinetry.

A unique cold pantry puts an end to stale crackers and chips and increases the shelf life of onions, potatoes, and citrus fruit.

Visiting an old 1920s farmhouse in the East, the owners fell in love with the idea of a root cellar. Disappointed that the water level in their western mountain valley prevented that, the idea of a cold pantry emerged.

"I wanted the ability to keep foods semi-chilled without refrigeration," Carney said, "and this solved the problem." A cold pantry has a low temperature adapted to keep produce, boxed cereals, and crackers fresh behind a heavily insulated latched door.

Made of cool gray soapstone, the efficiency of this masonry stove is unmatched by any metal one. It produces up to 60,000 BTUs/hour and radiates steady warmth over a long period of time. But touching the surface cannot burn a hand. The flue system causes it to consume its own gases, emitting less pollution. Complicated as it is to build, it's the picture of visual simplicity that is complemented by classic white tile found around the kitchen.

The upper crust of cooking ranges, this beautiful stove is unapproachable by any other. There is an air of professionalism in a warm homey setting. By La Cornue.

A La Cornue cooking range—seen in this country mostly in exclusive French magazine ads—is even finer looking in person. These cooking ranges are hand-assembled and made of cast iron, stainless steel, nickel, brass, and porcelain enamel. They evenly distribute heat, cooking food to perfection.

Throughout the house, the walls are plastered smooth up to the windows and doors and remain clean-looking with no wood trim. Yet there is a plethora of rich red mahogany everywhere. Crimson doors line the hallways, in contrast to the soft white walls ,and gloriously replicate the floors.

With closets and an island bureau in the master bath, one need go no farther to get dressed, with the shower and dressing room combined in one area.

Behind one of those doors, the master bath has adopted the idea of a central island cabinet usually found in kitchens. "I love having all my personal dressing items under my nose," says the owner. "I didn't want closets in our bedroom as the idea is to get dressed right out of the shower." The soft rich lighting throughout this oversized bathroom seldom disappoints those using the mirror.

The house is deeply personal, filled with fine antiques looking like family heirlooms that could have traveled the plains in a covered wagon. No one specific style can be identified. It's eclectic and has an ethereal quality,

binding it to the architecture. There is a sense of taming the West with elegance. The French-tapestry room screen in the master bedroom could very well be from a French castle, an armoire in the kitchen, Scandinavian. The furnishings were simply selected because they reflect the owner's taste and lifestyle.

No one in the family has thought twice about the decision to purchase the property spontaneously on a first ski trip. They now have the freedom of owning and riding horses, rock climbing, and, of course, unlimited skiing. ▼

CHAPTER SIX

THE HEALING POWERS of the Mountain

THE HEALING POWERS
of the Mountain

The family who owns this home believes in the healing powers of the mountains. When their little girl became seriously ill with a disease similar to rickets, a radical doctor told them to take her outside as much as possible. In retreat from the city, they took her to the Rocky Mountains and built a family life centered on outdoor activities. Today, she is married and has children of her own. With the regeneration of her health, the legacy has passed to another generation. To accommodate extended family gatherings, this commodious house with panoramic views fits their needs.

At first glance, there are only hints of the volume of space. Architect Gary Francis has ingeniously created a low-profile illusion with the design. Playing hide-and-seek with the mountain, bits of river stone, log timbers, and shake roof suggest a massive surprise on entry.

All the romance of traditional building materials is here, but the house is far from being a conspicuous log home. From the front, it looks barely one story, with a series of pitched rooflines rising from ground level. Subtle dormers give away the second story. In winter, the snow level nearly erases evidence of the house on the north side. The south-facing side is three stories and opens onto a ski run, but the structure hugs the hill as though a part of it.

The owners have an appreciation for handcrafted furniture. Whenever possible, they like to use local craftsmen. The main motif of the house is nature, evidenced by various furniture pieces and interior detailing. Finely woven branches line the ascending staircase, and natural twists and turns of a larger branch provide a railing for the descending stairs. This theme is most obvious in the entrance table. Whole tree trunks form the legs, holding the weighty table surface—one continuous piece of wood, four inches thick. The carved birds may not be seen right away, for they are not only up in a tree but also below eye level. Tactile and artistically interpreted by Jerzy S. Kennar in natural purple heart and creamy fossil ivory, they have nested in the branches of the mirror and the hollows in the legs.

Eating in this room, diners take in surrounding vistas while seated on a piece of art. A special finish has been applied over the carved wood of these chairs. Through a multiple process of gesso layered with paint, Gonzalo Tengono achieves a unique antique patina.

In the living room, the vaulted ceiling handles the scale of the massive river-stone fireplace with bravado and gives away the spacious secret beneath the peaked roofs. Fires are welcome in the fireplace on nights when temperatures can reach 20 degrees below zero. The lodge-sized chandelier diffuses light through leather parchment framed in steel. The room is filled with oversized sofas and chairs.

"The most important thing in the house is for family and guests to feel they are in a comfortable place—one where you can kick off your shoes, put your feet up and not feel guilty," says the owner. "We entertain a lot and want our guests, especially, to feel at home."

The couple is well traveled and picks up incredible carvings, crafts and arts that are now a feast for the eyes throughout the house. "These items personalize our home. Many objects here are gifts and reminders of a friend," she says, looking around the room. "It keeps the friendship forever alive."

A series of horses carved from a single tree trunk is a sinewy tower reaching skyward. Selected on a trip to Indonesia and shipped home, it is a multicultural match to a western lifestyle.

Located on the lower level of the house is a lap pool extraordinaire. Unlike many homes in which a pool would be merely a showpiece, this one is used every morning—a combination spa for the body and sanctuary for the soul. Keeping with the natural theme of the house, it is cast in grainy concrete, giving the appearance of a sandy bottom. It is an official Olympic-length pool, so there is no cheating on the number of laps completed.

Set up for a conversation area, one might easily get the urge to remove shoes and rest his or her feet on the leather coffee table/ottoman. It is an inviting spot for solving the world's problems or gazing quietly at a snowy garden. ▼

CHAPTER SEVEN

A "TREE" House

A "TREE" House

"This is one of the most difficult sites I have ever built on," architect Von White says. On a steep hill at a forty-five-degree angle, he opted not to use fill and pondered how to save two exceptionally large pine trees. As an outdoorsman, he came with his dogs to study the site, hoping the sunset would inspire him. The result: he drew three large Cs around one tree in his sketchbook. The other had to go. The house was so thoroughly thought out that it took two years to complete the drawings and three more to build it. As a multilayered complex, it steps down five stories at some points, and the pine tree can be seen from almost every room in the house.

Codes for mountain homes are strict and rigorous. For this mountain home, Von used large structural beams and steel framing to carry the snow. "Code requires the house carry a load of 180 pounds per square foot and that snow blow off one side."

At first he designed cozy log cabins, but there was a limit to the size of windows, and both he and his clients love light. In this contemporary home, he curved the glass to the views, being careful to keep the energy code in mind. "It's strict here because of heat loss. You must pick and choose where you put windows."

Because of his sensitivity to the environment, the quality of his structures, and his creativity, these homeowners were happy to find Von White. They had a huge hand in the design of the house and relished the personal attention from Von. "We chose the mountains because of nature, God's presence, and a sense of peace. When I look out the window, I see a painting," says the artist/owner. She likes to paint nature, and her style changed radically when they moved from the East. "The light is quite different here. The days start earlier—usually by 5 A.M. in the summer."

The interiors were also approached like a work of art. Each room represented a new canvas; yet she didn't want to compete with the outside "painting." When first stepping inside the house, one is immediately drawn to the mountain view perfectly framed in the two-story windows. Hung next to nature's painting is the owner's interpretation of God's aspen grove.

The house is full of gently rolling feminine curves in both structure and furnishings. "I didn't want sharp edges—rounded walls softened the house," she says with conviction. A crescent sofa in the living room is filled with the open arms of soft pillows, and the basic lines are complemented with special antiques that were gathered around the world.

The kitchen is no exception to the curved design found throughout this house. The crescent shapes fill the masculine volume with a feminine touch.

Curved counters in the kitchen create a natural flow that draws visitors into the warmth of a feast cooking on the stove. The copper of the stove hood turns an otherwise boring necessity into a work of art. Rich limestone counters and floor tiles are earthy and sumptuous at the same time. The breakfast bar invites guest or family member to comingle with the very sustenance of life, be it conversation with the cook or tasting what she is preparing.

Wine connoisseurs would be hard-pressed to find a more tasteful way to store their aged treasures. Sensitive to traditional wine-tasting ceremonies in Italy, the homeowners created authentically textured cellar walls that reflect a glowing buttery color in candlelight. The crowning tribute is a bronze sculptural railing of grapes and leaves, created by a Russian craftsman.

This room is a dream come true for any wine connoisseur with the temperature chilled just right to preserve the finest bottled treasures.

It's logical that the bed would be the focal point of the master bedroom, and that's where the owner started. The headboard was originally an antique hand-painted screen from Indonesia. Wes Wright, a fellow artist, helped turn a vision into reality by perfectly matching carved feet to the bedstead. The rest of the montage fell easily into place once the focal point was complete. "I am very detail-oriented—and detail provides the best opportunity to express that personal touch. In the end, it sets the house apart."

In this home office, thinkers are inspired by one of the finest collections of ancient Chinese pottery and artifacts.

In the study, a comprehensive collection of ancient Chinese pottery emanates the centuries of imagination that went into it. Windows with a view and an old English club chair provide a cozy corner for contemplation. The fireplace, again curved, is of chiseled limestone.

Such care in choosing special pieces extends to the patio. The deck chairs, once sea-bound on an elegant ocean liner, are now dry-docked for meditation over mountains. A former southern grain

grinder has been cleverly reincarnated into an artistic bench, and a stone-tile bowl from Indonesia now serves as a wine chiller at parties or naturally becomes a birdbath when not in use by humans. ▼

Wooden deck chairs from a 1930s ocean liner are retired to the serenity and stability of the mountains.

CHAPTER EIGHT

VICTORIAN Charm

Family heirlooms are reupholstered to suit modern needs in this contemporary Victorian living room. A Chinese poster from the 1930s is not out of place, as workers from China were instrumental in early mountain developments.

VICTORIAN
Charm

In most historic sections of silver-mining towns, a strict code preserves the architectural legacy of the 1800s, be it a miner's saltbox version or a Victorian manor. Minus the fluff and gingerbread of that era, this sophisticated house was built in the early 1970s on the cusp of the ski boom that ultimately revived the town.

"We came here for a slower pace. I worked in a Los Angeles office, and my husband came from Minnesota," the owner says wistfully. "There were a lot of college students here, looking for a simpler way of life. We all knew each other, and you could walk everywhere. We didn't even need to lock our door."

In the beginning, this Victorian was a smaller house for a bachelor who was a designer and building contractor. During a recent remodeling, a wraparound porch was added so the beauty of the valley and the splendor of the mountain could be enjoyed from an armchair. In addition, space was added to the living room and dining room for the new owners. The ceilings are a standard eight feet high, and the rooms have minimal square footage. This makes the house manageable for the owner's wife, and she likes it that way. "I like small cozy spaces where I can feel intimate with family and friends. And it's easy to clean."

The interior is best described as "nouveau Victorian." Reclaimed oak flooring provides a rich dark palette for the furnishings—an eclectic collection of antiques that suit the exterior. "My husband brought many of the pieces from Minnesota—the sofas and chairs have all been reupholstered," the owner says, gazing at the pieces as if they were family members. "The lounge upstairs came from my sister-in-law's drugstore attic. We didn't know it opened into a bed until we got the word from the upholsterer."

A 1920s Chinese poster hanging above a carved mantelpiece in the

living room adds to the historic atmosphere. Not far from the house, a Chinese community once bustled with enterprise—building steps on steep slopes, cooking in restaurants, and growing victory gardens. As if in remembrance of this past, an Asian trunk sits atop a chipped-paint cabinet, sharing the space with a Victorian lamp. Stylist and designer Eva Kline artfully combined eras and cultures with just the right accents and splashes of color to make the room interesting though uncluttered.

The nostalgic look of the country kitchen suits the needs of this contemporary family. Chipped-paint cabinets house a stainless-steel stove-top and oven. Waiting by the window is an inviting banquette where breakfast can be enjoyed while perusing the morning newspaper.

In the master bedroom, a contemporary version of molded tin graces the mahogany bedstead. Velvet pillows and duvet add soft color to the room. An antique oak nightstand is a protean companion piece for the bed.

Soft soothing earth tones invite the occupants to relax in a Jacuzzi tub by candlelight before retiring. The limestone floors of the master bath have a porous sand-textured feeling on bare feet. The corner shower door swings freely on double-hung stainless hinges, sturdy enough to hold the weight of half-inch glass. ▼

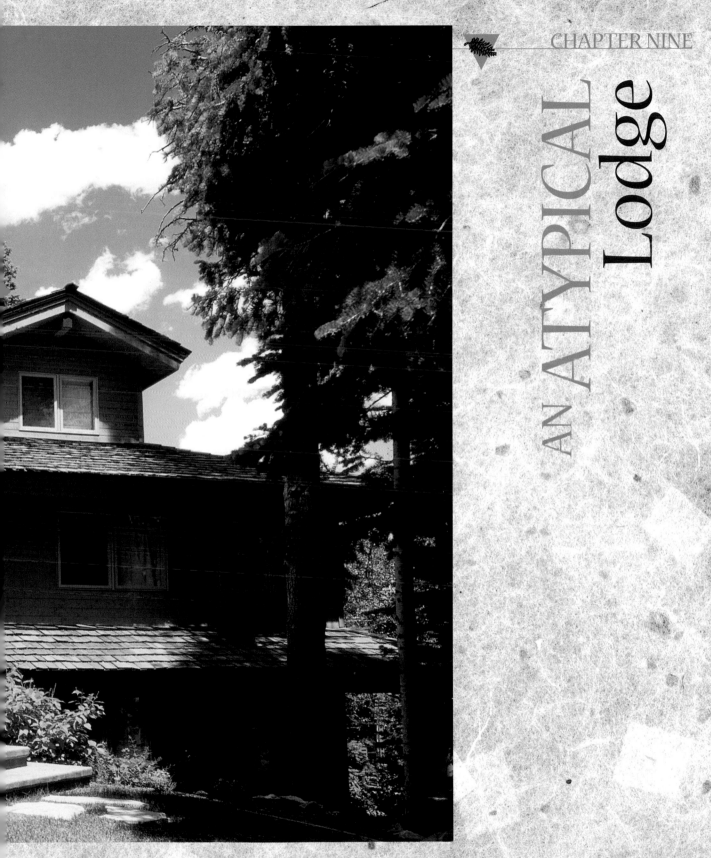

CHAPTER NINE

AN ATYPICAL Lodge

AN ATYPICAL
Lodge

The owners of this home were immediately taken by the straightforward design so unlike the typical lodge look. Called to the mountains by the geologic area more than the western legends, these owners are able to practically ski out their back door. The house is on a mountainside but hidden in the trees, blending their classic eastern lifestyle with civilized wilderness. As a family of four, the desire to recreate together was answered here. The children love to bike, hike, and ski—an inherited affinity for the outdoors shared with their parents.

Architect Gary Francis was hired to help personalize the house. "By the addition of windows and height, we were able to bring the outdoors inside," says the owner. "While adding light and an open feeling within, privacy was still maintained by the oversized pine trees."

Interior designer Tom Jones was aware the house needed to be comfortable and cozy for a large family. "Because of their four kids, they sometimes have eight or ten children join them. They like to sit around the fireplace and roast marshmallows. The furniture needed to be substantial." With these practical necessities in mind, along with the family's

gravitation toward modern art, Tom chose a multi-color palette of materials for the furnishings. Earth tones and textures for floor, ceilings, and walls complement both. The fine artistic lines of the Italian chairs around the dining table are slip-covered with leather. "The sumptuous leather is practical for kids—spills wipe up easily—no problem," says Jones.

Local furniture design team Ruth and John Sundberg crafted the dining room table from one re-sawn slab of koa wood, native only to Hawaii. The natural debarked edge varies from the color of the heartwood to that of the sapwood. One coat of natural Danish oil was applied over a finely sanded top and then it was finished with a tung-oil topcoat. A stainless-steel base blends the rugged with the refined. Koa is a rare wood, fiercely protected by government controls and is not always available.

The claro walnut used in the making of this writing table is found only in northern California near the border of Oregon. The trees are stately loners measuring up to fifty-four inches in diameter. The wood is rated by its "curl"—the tighter the curl, the higher the value. Simple in design, the frame-and-panel construction that John used was mitered at the corners as a finishing touch.

ABOVE: One slab of rare koa wood makes up this ten-foot dining room table crafted by Walrus Woodworking. Leather slipcovers are practical on these chairs; spills wipe up easily.

RIGHT: This simple claro walnut desk has a provocatively beautiful grain. The subtle half-round trim frames but doesn't distract from its beauty. By Walrus Woodworking.

Cheng Designs had a challenge with the kitchen space. Stuck in an alcove, the typical galley layout was embellished by the use of materials. The pre-cast concrete was poured off-site and installed in pieces. Random imprints of leaves were achieved with negative forms. The counters were *not* sealed to protect from stains. Alice Soohoo says, "Over the years, stains add to the patina layer upon layer. A coating would destroy the natural beauty."

The cabinet doors, made of Anegre and bird's-eye maple, have different grains going different directions, one of them in an offbeat color. Two sinks are possible with the luxury of a long counter—one for prep and one for cleanup. While the rest of the house has open high ceilings, they were lowered in the kitchen, creating cozy horizontal lines.

Alice Soohoo, of Fu Tung Cheng, designed this kitchen using a signature cast concrete on countertops and divider. It looks archeological with embossed leaves and a natural patina finish.

Existing rustic beams were wrapped in birch veneer, and a crazy mosaic of glass is embedded in a limestone floor tile. Free-form metal sculpture becomes a stair railing, with river stone surprisingly laced on acid-washed copper—nature, art, and function leading to a higher level.

Architectural lines of the concrete fireplace define the master bedroom. Pointed directly toward the outdoors, it leads the occupants' eyes to the trees. Diaphanous light filtering through curtain sheers is soothing to the eye, and makes reading in the contrasting red leather chair a pleasure. ▼

LEFT: The surprising use of red in this master bedroom invites the owners to escape here, using it as a private alternative to the living room.

OPPOSITE: A series of single chairs provide comfort, facing inward in a cozy conversation circle without excluding the warmth of the cast-concrete fireplace.

CHAPTER TEN

A LITTLE LOG CABIN in the Woods

A *LITTLE* LOG CABIN
in the Woods

For those who have dreamed of a *little* log cabin in the woods, this home might be the answer to that vision. In reality, it's an expanded version of that dream—somewhere between a one-room cabin and a national-park lodge. Most people have a certain nostalgia associated with the Wild West. This house satisfies the tradition of western history while suiting a contemporary lifestyle. The structure was a valid idea a hundred years ago, and it still makes sense today.

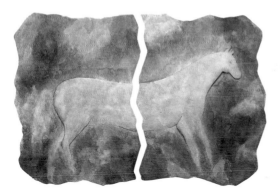

Log homes are based on common-sense building principles whereby the thickness of an entire tree trunk can nearly eliminate the need for framing and insulation. Chinking (now made of a latex-acrylic sealant that flexes with weather conditions) fills in the spaces between logs and creates an airtight exterior/interior wall. To divide rooms, some of the interior walls in this home are framed and plastered, creating a diverse departure and providing a backdrop for accessories. Simple wide-plank flooring adds warmth to the home and complements the walls. The home furnishings reflect an old-world European look that melds easily with aged timbers and river rock, placing the interior at ease with the exterior. This mix of styles reflects early ranches and pioneer homes.

"My clients want casual comfortable textures and colors, with a western influence here and there," says interior designer Brian Goff of Harker Designs. He knows the level of sophistication they live with in their primary residences. "We use a lot of high-end chenille fabrics and anything with texture in earthy color palettes. They are grounding colors and help people shed tension."

Many times, primary homes function in an atmosphere where daily lives are centered on the stress of maintaining family and career. Second homes are deliberately oriented toward recreation and are focused to satisfy that need.

"If furnishings have the patina of age, one is more apt to feel relaxed," Brian says, with the understanding of his craft. Harker Designs searches out case goods of European antiques from the Black Forest to France, Portugal, and England. What can't be found, they design and produce.

Variation in ceiling heights adds dimension to rooms that range from small and cozy to the great room, where larger groups of people can feel comfortable without being cramped.

Soft chenilles are tension breakers and earthy palettes are grounding colors. Four-inch cushions on small wood-frame chairs allow comfort without adding bulk.

In the early 1900s, the Scandinavian idea of winter recreation influenced the style of the lodges. Here the influence survives with a western overlay. By Harker Designs.

The conversation area is filled with furniture, so one feels embraced, invited to read, or induced to intimate conversation. The gentlemen's smoking chair is small in scale but fits the space well and hugs any occupant with ease. The courageous use of color in the rug adds vibrancy to the room, contrasting with the woody palette.

An old European-looking hutch has an Austrian feel to it. Although custom designed, it is destined to be a collectible. Created by Brian Goff, this piece has hand-carved oak branches along the top. On the door panels, a hand-painted mountain scene is embellished with hand carving as well.

The great room's three-story vaulted ceiling can handle the volume of fun in a room where a family entertains or plays games. The textured fabrics and patterned rug can easily camouflage what playful children might bring in from the outdoors on their shoes.

This reproduction of an antique French bed has a certain cultured polish in contrast to the alluring log backdrop—a refinement that courts old-world charm on Western terms.

In the master bedroom, an exquisite French antique-style bed tames the log timbers much the same as a family heirloom carried across the plains, while in the dining room, an Austrian-influenced grandfather clock watches over breakfast set for a round-table discussion. Barrel chairs are upholstered in leather and Indian-influenced geometric-patterned fabric—a prudent mixture of Old World and Native American. For formal dining these upholstered chairs are posturing for an evening of friendship and the ambrosia of a fine meal. A multitiered chandelier, reminiscent of an old English manor, highlights the solid-wood trestle table made of alder. ▼

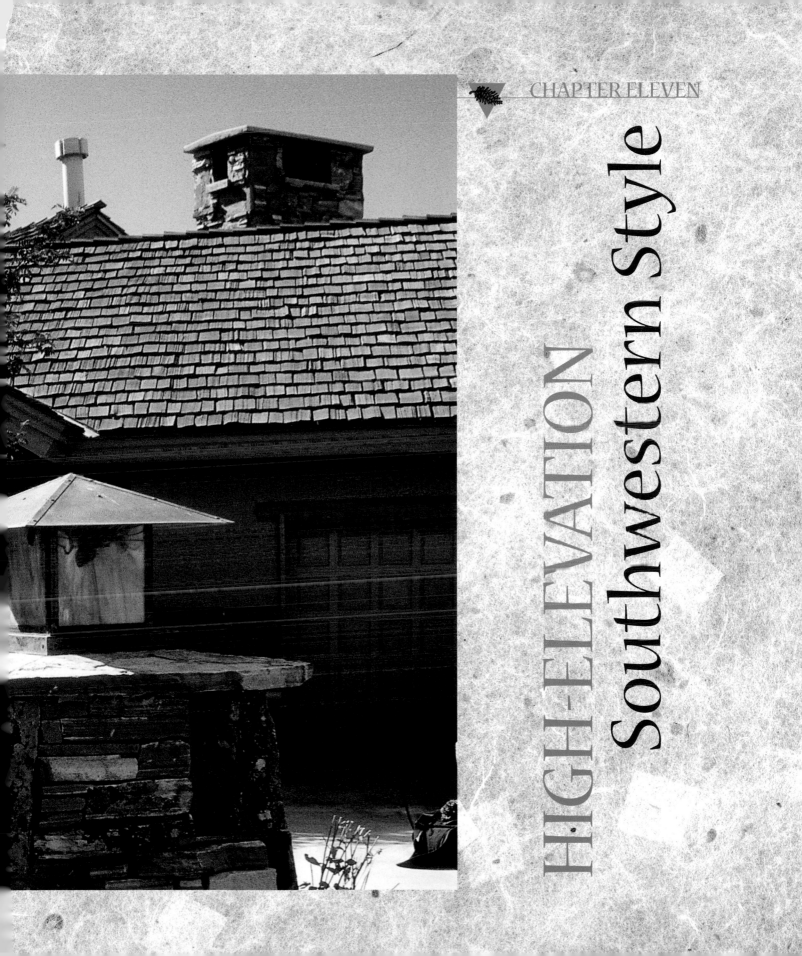

CHAPTER ELEVEN

HIGH-ELEVATION
Southwestern Style

HIGH-ELEVATION
Southwestern Style

When architect John Shirley was directed by his clients to combine several different styles into one harmonic convergence, a new style was coined: "high-elevation Southwestern style." Logs, Arts & Crafts, and southwestern blend together beautifully in this new style. "The home is wood-intensive, and we use a lot of wrought iron and bronze. It's a combination that works well," says Shirley.

The exterior red sandstone is unusual. Originally used on a turn-of-the-century chapel in Paris, Idaho, a quarry in Bear Lake, Utah, provided the stone for the 1910 church. The mason, Randy Borelin, convinced the quarry to provide stone for two contemporary homes. After doing the mason this favor, the quarry closed again shortly after the home was built. The variation in stone is as unpredictable as Mother Nature and ranges from lichen-covered surface quarry to cleaner subsurface stone. Randy used an Anasazi lay—some stones laid on their sides and some on edge in a dry-stack look.

There is a sense of attention to detail on the interior finishes. The simple Arts & Crafts cabinets, the wrought-iron hardware, and Craftsman fixtures complement the sandstone floors. The spectacular two-story stained-glass window in the hallway was patterned after an Indian blanket.

"You need to remember that geometric shapes cross over from Indian to Frank Lloyd Wright to Arts & Crafts. That makes a project like this a lot of fun. All those elements can be redefined, and our own interpretation makes it original," Shirley says, relishing the challenge.

A formal living room achieves dimension with a vaulted ceiling yet maintains intimacy in the seating area. The tufted ottoman/coffee table is multipurpose.

The stained-glass window wraps the soul with color, ever changing with the light of day. The geometric pattern pays homage to the Craftsman fixtures flanking both sides.

The red sandstone on the fireplace invites the exterior in to enliven the room with color and harmony. A Craftsman look ties nicely to the ancient dry-stack methods of the Anasazi. An old English club chair upholstered in timeworn leather suggests Hemingway may have sat there.

Classic upholstered dining room chairs are surprisingly distinguished by cutwork near the legs. The solid-wood table seats eight easily beneath the Craftsman chandelier. ▼

CHAPTER TWELVE

NATURE'S
Garden

NATURE'S
Garden

If one flower were to be singled out as the defining symbol of the Rocky Mountains, it would be columbine.

Delicate as an orchid in appearance, it is a hardy alpine flower that thrives in the harsh conditions of radical weather at high altitudes. All flowering plants are, or have been, wildflowers in one place or another throughout the world. Wild columbine found its way here from the alpine mountains of Europe. In fact, thanks to a strong interest in horticulture and healing herbs in the seventeenth century, European plant explorers transported flowers and herbs back and forth between continents. In addition, pioneers and settlers brought seeds and root starts that sometimes blew off wagons into fields or were left planted firmly along a trail by a muddy wheel or soil clinging to boots.

Columbine could well be known as the edelweiss of the western Rocky Mountains. Beautiful as an orchid, its delicate-looking petals are deceiving, for they propagate as easily as a dandelion.

OPPOSITE: Mother Nature, who resurrects multi-versions of this same garden in all its glory every July, easily takes care of God's wildflower garden. Species reside peacefully alongside one another for much of the summer. The grass never needs mowing; the flowers are neither pruned nor fertilized by man, yet they thrive. The petals are fresh, the colors vibrant, and they are drought tolerant. To man's credit, wildflower-seed mix allows humans to duplicate these scenes around their family homes.

Thousands of species from Europe have adapted to harsh winds, erratic water supply, and drastic temperature changes known here as Zones 2 through 4. Herbaceous perennials and

This parry primrose is rare and found only in avalanche paths. Horticulturists have tried but failed to cultivate the mysterious conditions that give birth to this species.

Yellow daisies seek refuge amongst fallen branches. They can grow thick and lush here, protected from nature's wrath.

bulbs thrive under a protective blanket of winter snow and become open fields of abundant color in late June and early July. Other flowers that are not as hardy adapt themselves to a microclimate around warm stones or among fallen trees. One particular flower, the parry primrose, grows only in avalanche paths and resists cultivation.

Plant growth varies from semiarid plains where grasses thrive, to mountain forests filled with aspen, fir, spruce, and pine, to the upland meadows where columbine, penstemon, and tiny coralbells flourish. Grasses are continually becoming more acceptable as an asset in cultivated gardens. They are hardy, grow easily, and require little to no maintenance.

Deliberately planted tree gardens mimic nature's wilderness in one's own backyard. Trees form a hierarchy of root systems. Aspens have shallow ones that continually search out water during a certain life cycle. Eventually, pine and fir choke them out and the aspens move on like migrating mountain men.

Nature, as its own gardener, continually alters and hybridizes plants, through cross-pollination, into other species. Many times this produces a feeble modification, and the new plant is weak because it can't produce plants like itself. This is the point where man becomes key. As a horticultural scientist, he has learned to propagate asexually from stem, leaf, or root cuttings, causing the recombination of genes.

One of nature's more beautiful wildflowers, purple lupine is hardy and prolific in the Rocky Mountains. Establishing roots deep within grassy meadows or steep slopes, it endures season after season.

This English-garden atmosphere allows the owner to cultivate flowers otherwise threatened by short growing seasons and cold nights. Sandwiched between a low stone wall and the stone facade of the house, these phlox and clovers benefit from stone's heat retention properties. In addition, the white gravel reflects sunlight and heat, helping maintain a constant bloom from a variety of annuals or perennials.

Gardens have changed and evolved over the years in the Rocky Mountains, from boomtowns to recreational resorts. Some have successfully reinvented cottage gardens; others have even coaxed herbs and vegetables to thrive in short seasons. But the most successful and beloved gardens are those grown from deliberately cast wildflower seeds.

"The majority of residents in the Rocky Mountains want an alpine look in their gardens with little to no maintenance," says landscape artist Gregg Bauman. "People want nature in their backyard, and that's what we specialize in." He advises his clients to "keep it simple, analyze the site, and try to mirror Mother Nature."

Grasses once thought of as a nuisance have found their way into controlled landscape schemes. Here, confined in a stone planter, they need little to no upkeep and provide an artistic foreground to a spectacular mountainscape.

No one wants to be married to gardening, yet one wants the tranquility a garden provides. Baby boomers watched parents manicure lawns and flower beds, but they don't want to do the same. Time and freedom have become precious hours to spend with their children sharing outdoor activities such as fishing, biking, hiking, and skiing.

Being a lazy gardener is a realistic option in the mountains, and seed companies have made it easy. A variety of wildflower mixes can be sprinkled from cans as a random act of planting in the spring or fall. Add a bit of fertilizer, cover with a thin layer of moss, and water. To enjoy this method, one must be willing to be surprised. "Try to avoid a mix with yarrow," Gregg advises. "It's like a kudzu that will take over and choke out all the other flowers in time."

This natural-looking forest of spruce trees was actually brought in full size and planted. Profoundly close to the work of Mother Nature, they have survived where none have grown naturally.

Other hardy plants that will withstand harsh winter snows and drought conditions are lilac bushes, chokecherry, tulips, daffodils, and crocus. Bushes and trees with colorful leaves such as amur, Rocky Mountain maple, yellow flowering potentilla, flowering crab apple, Canadian red chokecherry, and aspen prolong the look of color into late fall. Once gardeners start planting such shrubs and trees, they begin to get away from a willy-nilly type of landscape and into planned **plant-hood**.

Ivy grows in most climates. It is a prolific and aggressive filler. Here it softens this massive stone retaining wall, framing the hard surface with softness. It will eventually cover the metal trellis and will need to be contained and cut back at intervals to make it conform to the desired shape.

Well-traveled mountain citizens are often taken with the landscape artistry at fine hotels. They come home wanting to duplicate the botanical virtuosity experienced on vacation, seeing it as a formula for tranquility and soul renewal on a daily basis. But care and upkeep become more of a science in difficult elevated conditions. Selecting the right plant types is a must if one wishes to avoid pruning, cutting, and overwatering. Plants can be manipulated to fit the environment. Ornamental cherry trees, lavender, phlox, poppies, and ivy are a few. Brick and rock walls protect plants and help carry them through the winter, making it possible to have a cottage garden in the mountains.

Water is the ultimate feature in a yard that can bring equanimity. Ponds, waterfalls, water fountains, and creeks can massage away the day's stress and restore balance to our perspective on life. Sophisticated cleansing systems

are now available to generate the right environment for brook trout. Pumps and rubberized materials that don't tear have taken the place of concrete that shrinks and cracks.

"I know an artist who loves to look out onto her pond surrounded by a host of colors," says Gregg, who specializes in water features. "It inspires her paintings. She also has a waterfall that cuts street noise and quiets demons."

Mimicking natural mountain waterfalls that tumble over huge boulders is a monstrous task, but using such boulders doesn't stop Gregg. He uses large machinery to gather and place mammoth stones on private grounds to duplicate such falls. The effect is dramatic, placing raw nature at man's backdoor. Controlling evaporation of running water, which is normally around 2 percent, can be a problem in drought seasons. Draining recycled water into a storage vault while not in use minimizes the problem. Sensors installed in the driveway can turn on a waterfall feature when the owner arrives home.

Some of the biggest pleasures of living in the Rocky Mountains are the mountain streams and unexpected waterfalls found around the curve in a hiking trail. Now bringing nature into one's own backyard is an option. With the right equipment, boulders and stones can be moved and placed to mimic nature's water show. Recycled water with new rubberized blad systems conserves water without sacrificing the cascade. Strategically placed lighting prolongs the seduction of falling waters into the night. A stone staircase allows closer interaction with the bubbles and over-sprays. Plants and shrubbery provide fill, eventually allowing Mother Nature to complete the setting.

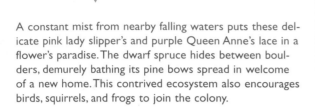

A constant mist from nearby falling waters puts these delicate pink lady slipper's and purple Queen Anne's lace in a flower's paradise. The dwarf spruce hides between boulders, demurely bathing its pine bows spread in welcome of a new home. This contrived ecosystem also encourages birds, squirrels, and frogs to join the colony.

OPPOSITE: Flower boxes framing windows make home part of garden. Contained plants proliferate in a secure atmosphere and the blooms have greater longevity.

ABOVE: Using garden sculpture such as this wheelbarrow adds character and dimension to the area.

BELOW: This fountain is strategically located near the gazebo so that a trickle of water can be heard, creating a perfect setting for relaxation.

When effort like this has been put into landscaping and planting, care of it is essential. Different levels of gardening require different levels of upkeep. As discussed above, wildflower gardens are for those who enjoy the loose random look of nature that needs little human care. Planned and cultivated gardens need regular care. Fertilize in the spring and fall with slow-release granules. Although bugs are few in mountain environments, pests should be watched for and treated. Most of all, a healthy garden is a painting for the soul and maintenance aid for one's sanity. ▼

This ground cover is a glorious visual alternative to a care-intensive lawn, especially nice in small patches between sidewalk and driveway where mowing is difficult.

Working in color schemes with flowers and planters can create a dramatic effect. This unusual concrete planter with chipped pink paint will complement various shades of flowers ranging from bright pink to purple-pink and pastels. The lush plump blossoms on this cultivated lupine are hardier than the wildflower version and can be planted in clumps and controlled in a flower bed.

To man's credit, poppies have been hybridized into colors and sizes beyond their natural glory. This field poppy produces seed pods that can be traded with a neighbor. The medium-sized poppy resembles the colossal Asian type in color and shape but doesn't approach its size.

Architects

Carney Architects
Nancy Carney
215 South King Street
Jackson Hole, WY 83002
(307) 733-5546

G. F. & A.
Gary Francis & Associates
Gary Francis
1821 Sidewinder Drive
Park City, UT 84060
(435) 649-7168

JSA
John C. Shirley, Architect
3115 Lion Lane #200
Salt Lake City, UT 84111
(801) 278-8151

Von M. White, AIA
333 South 300 East
Salt Lake City, UT 84102
(801) 364-7831

Interior Designers

Calvin & Lloyd
Tom Jones
140 Granby Street
Norfolk, VA 23509
(757) 616-1742

Fu Tung Cheng
Alice Soohoo
Margarit Burnett
Jason Lopez
2808 San Pablo Avenue
Berkeley, CA 94702
(510) 849-3272

Juidiith Clawson & Associates
Juidiith Clawson
2257 South 1100 East
Salt Lake City, UT 84105
(801) 468-0528
(801) 468-0527 fax

The Flying Trunk
Eva Klein
408 Main Street
P.O. Box 3537
Park City, UT 84060
(435) 649-0514

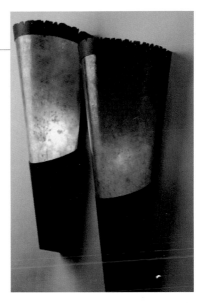

Harker Designs
Pat Harker
Brian Goff
3445 North Pines Way
Wilson, WY 83002
(307) 733-5960
(208) 523-3323

Marilyn Lewis Interior Design
Marilyn Lewis
1817 East 3300 South
Salt Lake City, UT 84106
(801) 466-6086

Natural Instincts
Jo Ann Mullen
1300 Snow Creek Drive
Suite P/Q
Park City, UT 84060
(435) 645-7635

Mary Whitesides
P.O. Box 2189
Park City, UT 84060
(435) 649-7249
(435) 655-3279 fax

Craftsmen

Art Shoppe
Collectors Gallery
Reproductions
2131 Yonge Street
Toronto, ON M4S 2A7
CANADA
(416) 487-3211
(416) 487-3221 fax

Hugh C. Culley
P.O. Box 522002
Salt Lake City, UT 84103
(801) 975-9314

El Paso Import Co.
Rustic Furniture
Jack Delaney
2225 Mills Street
El Paso, TX 79901
(915) 532-6531

Hammerton
Steve Young
2150 South 3675 West #3
West Valley City, UT 84120

Metal Sculpture
Cordell Taylor
575 West 200 South
Salt Lake City, UT 84102
(801) 355-0333

Red Rose Antiques
Architectural iron
Stained-glass windows
4285 Main Street
Vancouver, BC V5V 3P8
CANADA
(604) 875-8588

Sculpted Glass
Frank Quist
2640 South 3rd West
Salt Lake City, UT 84103
(801) 277-3363

Sculptor
Dennis Smith
11055 Gambol
Highland, UT 84003
(801) 756-5463

Tru Craft Log Specialties
P.O. Box 29
Site 3, RR #3
Lacombe, AB l0C 1S0
CANADA
(402) 782-5544

Vintage Arts LTD.
Furniture Refinishing
Carl Timm
3774 South 2300 East
Salt Lake City, UT 84104
(801) 277-5253

Walrus Woodworking
Ruth & John Sundberg
4748 North Highway 189
Oakley, UT 84055
(435) 486-8055

Western Iron Makers
Loren Brady
1105 South 1680 West
Orem, UT 84105
(801) 224-7320

Wooden Gallery Studio
Jerzy S. Kennar
1007–15 North Wolcott
Chicago, IL 60622
(312) 324-2550

Home Furnishings

Aid to Artisans
331 Wethersfield Avenue
3rd Floor
Hartford, CT 06114
(860) 947-3344

Alteriors Home
Furnishings + Design
527 Danforth Avenue
Toronto, ON M4S 2A7
CANADA
(416) 466-3622

Judi Boisson
Quilts
134 Mariner Drive
Southampton, NY 11968
(631) 283-5466

The Flying Trunk
Eva Klein
408 Main Street
P.O. Box 3537
Park City, UT 84060
(435) 649-0514

Great Pacific Woodworks
Carved-wood boxes and furniture
3495 Cambie Street #169
Vancouver, BC V5Z 4R3
CANADA

Hammerton
Steve Young
2150 South 3675 West #3
West Valley City, UT 84120
(801) 973-8095

Harker Designs Showroom
Brian Goff
3445 North Pines Way
Wilson, WY 83002
(307) 733-5960

Keramics
Dinnerware
Charo Elonzo
Av. Angamon Est. 346
Lima 18
PERU

Dave LaMure Jr.
Lamps and Pottery
3307 East 3200 North
Kimberly, ID 83341
(208) 736-9845

Magnolia Teak
Steamer Chairs/Lounges
Toronto, ON M4S 2A7
CANADA
(416) 922-2785

Mica Lamp Company
Ralph P. Ribicic, President
517 State Street
Glendale, CA 91203
(818) 241-7227

Napiers Antiques
Leather Club Chairs
   (1930s to 1990s)
Hardware
67430-96 216th Street
Langley, BC V0X 1T0
CANADA

Mailing:
Box 59
Milner, BC X0X 1T0
CANADA
(604) 534-7222
(604) 534-7223 fax

Natural Instincts
Jo Ann Mullen
1300 Snow Creek Drive
Suite P/Q
Park City, UT 84060
(435) 645-7635

Palecek
Darcy Bock Forman
10036 North 27th Place
Phoenix, AZ 86028
(480) 837-5205

Pinetree Furniture
Gerry Porter
1721 Hillside at Shelbourne
Vancouver, BC V8P 1A2
CANADA
(250) 595-2800

Pinto Pony Designs
361 South Main Street
Heber, UT 84603
(435) 654-5555

Sarita Furniture
Outdoor Furniture
2393 Old Nanaimo Highway
Box 1269
Port Alberni, BC V9Y 7MI
CANADA
(888) 472-7482
(250) 723-1967 fax
moreinfo@saritafurniture.net

Sundance Catalog Company
3865 West 1400 South
Salt Lake City, UT 84120
(801) 973-2711

Mary Whitesides
P.O. Box 2189
Park City, UT 84060
(435) 649-7249
(435) 655-3279 fax

Wynans Furniture and
Upholstery
Custom Furniture
4573 Merrifield Street
Port Alberni BC V97 6R5
CANADA
(250) 724-2021
(250) 724-7333 fax
artwynans@telus.net

Mountain Gardens

Bauman Design
Gregg Bauman
4091 East Quarry Drive
Sandy, UT 84092
(801) 694-2588
(800) 318-3813 toll-free

flow-er hard-ware
Cecilia Heffernan
3445 North Pines Way
Space 103
Wilson, WY 83002
(307) 733-7040

Curtis Tanner Association
Landscape Architect
331 Rio Grande, Suite 302
Salt Lake City, UT 84101
(801) 355-0631

Yank Azman
Antique Luggage (accessories)
Harbor Front Antiques Market
390 Queens Quay
Toronto, ON M4S 2A7
CANADA
(877) 260-5662

Craftsmen in Wood
Manufacturing
Interior Doors and Hardware
4040 W. Whitton Avenue
Phoenix, AZ 85019
(602) 278-8054

Heating Research Company
David Lyle
Acworth Road
Acworth, NH 03601

La Cornue Soapstone Stoves
Purcell Murray Inc.
La Cornue Cooking Ranges
113 Parklane
P.O. Box 83
Brisbane, CA 94005
(800) 892-4040 toll-free

Masonry Heater Association
of North America
Masonry Stoves
Dave Holland
P.O. Box 669
Englewood, CO 80151

Tulikivi
Soapstone Stoves
P.O. Box 83
Pray, MT 59065
(406) 333-4383
info@warmstone.com

Contractors

Barndt Construction
P.O. Box 3984
Park City, UT 84060
(801) 649-9730

Chappell Construction
Lewis Chappell
932 Lake Creek Way
Heber, UT 84032
(435) 654-3997

Miscellaneous

A-Lite Custom Window & Door
Patio Doors & Wood Windows
2212 South West Temple
Salt Lake City, UT 84115
(801) 487-4440

Aquatech
Exterior Spa
3075 South Main
Salt Lake City, UT 84115

Bibliography

The following pamphlets, books, and articles were used as reference material:

Barlow-Perez, Sally. *A History of Aspen*, 2nd edition. Basalt, Colorado: Who Press, 2000.

Circumerro, Steve. *The Jackson Hole Guest Directory Rendezvous*. Jackson Hole, Wyoming: Circumerro Publishing, 1999.

Daughters of the Utah Pioneers-Summit County. *Echos of Yesterday*. Salt Lake City, Utah: Mountain States Bindery, 1947.

Hayen, Elizabeth Wide. *From Trapper to Tourist in Jackson Hole*. Jackson Hole, Wyoming: Grand Teton Natural History Association, 1992.

Johnson, Lady Bird, and Carlton B. Lees. *Wildflowers Across America*. New York, New York: Abbeville Press, Inc., 1988.

Owens, Harry J. *Characters of the Past*. Livingston, Montana: Livingston Enterprises, 1989.

Ringholz, Rya C. *Diggings & Doings in Park City*, 5th edition. Park City, Utah: Raye Carlson Ringholz, 1983.

Seabolt, Stephen J. *Sunset Western Landscaping*. Menlo Park, California: Sunset Books, 1997.

Thompson, George A., and Fraser Buck. *Treasure Mountain Home*. Salt Lake City, Utah: Dream Garden Press, 1993.

Zupan, Shirley. *History of Red Lodge*. Red Lodge, Montana: Shirley Zupan, 1989.

Photographic Credits

All photographs are by and copyright © 2001 by
Matthew Reier with the exception of the following:

Gregg Bauman
Pages 10, 114, 115, 116, and 121

Judi Boisson
Page 35

Country Originals
Page 79

David LaMure
Page 59

Hammerton
Pages 12, 18, and 29

JHHSM
(Jackson Hole Historical Society and Museum)
Page 18

Martin Harris Gallery
Page 97

The Mica Lamp Company
Pages 137 and 138

Palacek
Pages 13, 34, and 138

Sundance Catalog Company
Opposite title page, and pages 27, 28, 33, 47,
and 87

Park City Historical Society
John Sneedlove Collection
Page 21

Paul Winder
Pages 117, 120, and 121

Mary Whitesides
Pages 116, 118, 119, 122, 123, 127, 128, 131,
132, and 135